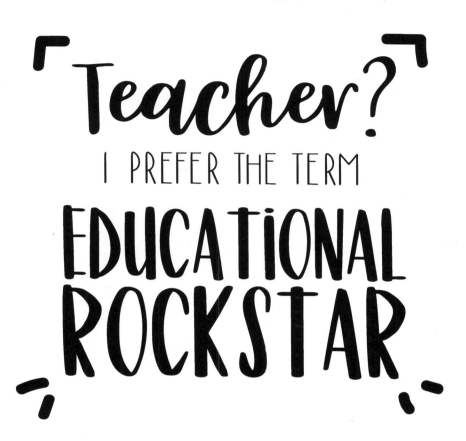

THIS BOOK BELONGS TO:

_____

Teacher Planner Lesson Planner
©Pretty Simple Planners. All rights reserved. No part of this publication may be reproduced, distributed, or transmitted, in any form or by any means, including photocopying, recording, or other electronic or mechanical methods, without prior written permission of the publisher, except in the case of brief quotations embodied in critical reviews and certain other noncommercial uses permitted by copyright law.

IMPORTANT DATES

January
NEW YEAR'S DAY
MARTIN LUTHER KING DAY

February
GROUNDHOG DAY
VALENTINE'S DAY
PRESIDENTS DAY

March
ST. PATRICK'S DAY

July
INDEPENDENCE DAY

August

September
LABOR DAY

April
APRIL FOOL'S DAY
EARTH DAY

May
CINCO DE MAYO
MOTHER'S DAY
MEMORIAL DAY

June
FATHER'S DAY

October
COLUMBUS DAY
HALLOWEEN

November
VETERANS DAY
THANKSGIVING

December
HANUKKAH
CHRISTMAS EVE
CHRISTMAS DAY
NEW YEAR'S EVE

July 2018

SUNDAY	MONDAY	TUESDAY	WEDNESDAY
1	2	3	4 INDEPENDENCE DAY
8	9	10	11
15 *National Ice Cream Day*	16	17	18
22	23 *National Hot Dog Day*	24	25
29	30	31	

[If you ask me what I came into this life to do, I will tell you: I came to live out loud.
-Émile Zola]

THURSDAY	FRIDAY	SATURDAY	NOTES
5	6	7	
12	13	14	
19	20	21	
26	27	28	

WEEK OF _____	Monday	Tuesday
SUBJECT:		

Wednesday	Thursday	Friday

WEEK OF _____	Monday	Tuesday
SUBJECT:		

Wednesday	Thursday	Friday

WEEK OF _____

SUBJECT:

Monday

Tuesday

Wednesday	Thursday	Friday

WEEK OF _____	Monday	Tuesday
SUBJECT:		

Wednesday	Thursday	Friday

August 2018

SUNDAY	MONDAY	TUESDAY	WEDNESDAY
			1
5	6	7	8
	Root Beer Float Day		
12	13	14	15
19	20	21	22
26	27	28	29

> The secret of getting ahead is getting started.
> - Mark Twain

THURSDAY	FRIDAY	SATURDAY	NOTES
2	3	4	
9	10	11	
16	17	18	
Tell A Joke Day			
23	24	25	
30	31		

WEEK OF 8/7 - 8/10	Monday	Tuesday
SUBJECT: 2A - Art 1		8/7 2A Art 1 - Expectations - Who R U Ques.
3A - Photo		8/7 - Exp - WRU
4A - Photo		8/7 - Exp - WRU
1B - Photo		
2B - Art 1		
3B - Photo		

Wednesday	Thursday	Friday
	8/9 2A Art 1 - About Me Short Essay - M&M Game	
	8/9 - Short Essay - M&M Game	
	8/9 - '' -	
8/8 - EXP - WRU		8/11 ← ''
8/8 ''		
8/8 ''		

WEEK OF _____

SUBJECT:	Monday	Tuesday
	8/5 Art 1 - About Me Photo Essay - M&M game	
	8/6 - Short Essay - M&M game	
	8/7	
	8/8 "	8/8 - Exp - WRJ
		8/8 "
		8/9 "

Wednesday	Thursday	Friday

WEEK OF _____	Monday	Tuesday
SUBJECT:		

Wednesday	Thursday	Friday

WEEK OF _____

SUBJECT:

Monday

Tuesday

Wednesday	Thursday	Friday

WEEK OF _____	Monday	Tuesday
SUBJECT:		

Wednesday	Thursday	Friday

September 2018

SUNDAY	MONDAY	TUESDAY	WEDNESDAY
2	3 LABOR DAY	4	5
9	10 ROSH HASHANAH	11	12
16	17	18	19 YOM KIPPUR
23 / 30	24	25	26

[With the new day comes new strength and new thoughts.
— Eleanor Roosevelt]

THURSDAY	FRIDAY	SATURDAY
		1
6	7	8
Read a Book Day		
13	14	15
20	21	22
27	28	29
	Good Neighbor Day	

NOTES
_____
_____
_____
_____
_____
_____
_____
_____
_____
_____
_____
_____
_____
_____
_____
_____
_____
_____
_____
_____
_____
_____
_____

WEEK OF _____	Monday	Tuesday
SUBJECT:		

Wednesday	Thursday	Friday

WEEK OF _____	Monday	Tuesday
SUBJECT:		

Wednesday	Thursday	Friday

WEEK OF _____	Monday	Tuesday
SUBJECT:		

Wednesday	Thursday	Friday

WEEK OF _____	Monday	Tuesday
SUBJECT:		

Wednesday	Thursday	Friday

October 2018

SUNDAY	MONDAY	TUESDAY	WEDNESDAY
	1	2	3
7	8 COLUMBUS DAY	9	10
14	15	16	17
21	22	23	24
28	29	30	31 HALLOWEEN

[Simplicity is the keynote of all true elegance.
— Coco Chanel]

THURSDAY	FRIDAY	SATURDAY	NOTES
4 National Taco Day	5 World Smile Day	6	
11	12	13	
18	19	20	
25	26	27	

WEEK OF _____	Monday	Tuesday
SUBJECT:		

Wednesday	Thursday	Friday

WEEK OF _____	Monday	Tuesday
SUBJECT:		

Wednesday	Thursday	Friday

WEEK OF _____	Monday	Tuesday
SUBJECT:		

Wednesday	Thursday	Friday

WEEK OF _____	Monday	Tuesday
SUBJECT:		

Wednesday	Thursday	Friday

WEEK OF _____	Monday	Tuesday
SUBJECT:		

Wednesday	Thursday	Friday

november 2018

SUNDAY	MONDAY	TUESDAY	WEDNESDAY
4 DAYLIGHT SAVINGS ENDS	5	6	7
11 VETERANS DAY	12	13 *World Kindness Day*	14
18	19	20	21
25	26	27	28 *french Toast Day*

[The purpose of our lives is to be happy.
- Dalai Lama]

THURSDAY	FRIDAY	SATURDAY	NOTES
1	2	3	
8	9	10 *Vanilla Cupcake Day*	
15	16	17	
22 THANKSGIVING	23	24	
29	30		

WEEK OF _____	Monday	Tuesday
SUBJECT:		

Wednesday	Thursday	Friday

WEEK OF _____	Monday	Tuesday
SUBJECT:		

Wednesday	Thursday	Friday

WEEK OF _____	Monday	Tuesday
SUBJECT:		

Wednesday	Thursday	Friday

WEEK OF _____	Monday	Tuesday
SUBJECT:		

Wednesday	Thursday	Friday

December 2018

SUNDAY	MONDAY	TUESDAY	WEDNESDAY
2	3 **HANUKKAH**	4	5
9	10	11	12
16	17	18	19
23 / 30	CHRISTMAS EVE 24 / 31 NEW YEAR'S EVE	25 CHRISTMAS DAY	26 KWANZAA

[What is done in love is done well.
- Vincent Van Gogh]

THURSDAY	FRIDAY	SATURDAY	NOTES
		1	
6	7	8	
13	14	15	
20	21	22	
27	28	29	

WEEK OF _____	Monday	Tuesday
SUBJECT:		

Wednesday	Thursday	Friday

WEEK OF _____	Monday	Tuesday
SUBJECT:		

Wednesday	Thursday	Friday

WEEK OF _____	Monday	Tuesday
SUBJECT:		

Wednesday	Thursday	Friday

WEEK OF _____	Monday	Tuesday
SUBJECT:		

Wednesday	Thursday	Friday

January 2019

SUNDAY	MONDAY	TUESDAY	WEDNESDAY
		1 NEW YEAR'S DAY	2
6	7	8	9
13	14	15	16
20	21 MARTIN LUTHER KING JR. DAY	22	23 *National Pie Day*
27	28	29	30

[Nothing is impossible, the word itself says 'I'm possible'!
- Audrey Hepburn]

THURSDAY	FRIDAY	SATURDAY	NOTES
3	4	5	
10	11	12	
17	18	19 *National Popcorn Day*	
24	25	26	
31			

WEEK OF _____	Monday	Tuesday
SUBJECT:		

Wednesday	Thursday	Friday

WEEK OF _____	Monday	Tuesday
SUBJECT:		

Wednesday	Thursday	Friday

WEEK OF _____	Monday	Tuesday
SUBJECT:		

Wednesday	Thursday	Friday

WEEK OF _____	Monday	Tuesday
SUBJECT:		

Wednesday	Thursday	Friday

WEEK OF _____	Monday	Tuesday
SUBJECT:		

Wednesday	Thursday	Friday

february 2019

SUNDAY	MONDAY	TUESDAY	WEDNESDAY
3	4	5	6
10	11 *Make a Friend Day*	12	13
17	18 PRESIDENTS' DAY	19	20
24	25	26	27

[I have found if you love life, life will love you back.
— Arthur Rubinstein]

THURSDAY	FRIDAY	SATURDAY	NOTES
	1	2	_____
7	8	9	_____
14 VALENTINE'S DAY	15	16	_____
21	22	23	_____
28			_____

WEEK OF _____	Monday	Tuesday
SUBJECT:		

Wednesday	Thursday	Friday

WEEK OF _____	Monday	Tuesday
SUBJECT:		

Wednesday	Thursday	Friday

WEEK OF _____	Monday	Tuesday
SUBJECT:		

Wednesday	Thursday	Friday

WEEK OF _____	Monday	Tuesday
SUBJECT:		

Wednesday	Thursday	Friday

March 2019

SUNDAY	MONDAY	TUESDAY	WEDNESDAY
3	4	5	6
10	11	12	13
17 DAYLIGHT SAVINGS BEGINS	18	19	20
24 / 31 ST. PATRICK'S DAY	25	26	27

[Anything can happen if you let it.
- Mary Poppins]

THURSDAY	FRIDAY	SATURDAY	NOTES
	1	2	
7	8	9	
14	15	16	
National Pi Day			
21	22	23	
28	29	30	

WEEK OF _____	Monday	Tuesday
SUBJECT:		

Wednesday	Thursday	Friday

WEEK OF _____	Monday	Tuesday
SUBJECT:		

Wednesday	Thursday	Friday

WEEK OF _____	Monday	Tuesday
SUBJECT:		

Wednesday	Thursday	Friday

WEEK OF _____	Monday	Tuesday
SUBJECT:		

Wednesday	Thursday	Friday

April 2019

SUNDAY	MONDAY	TUESDAY	WEDNESDAY
	1	2	3
7	8	9	10 *National Siblings Day*
14	15	16	17
21 EASTER	22 EARTH DAY	23	24
28	29	30	

[The world belongs to the enthusiastic.
- Ralph Waldo Emerson]

THURSDAY	FRIDAY	SATURDAY	NOTES
4	5	6	
11	12	13	
18	19 GOOD FRIDAY	20	
25	26	27	

WEEK OF _____	Monday	Tuesday
SUBJECT:		

Wednesday	Thursday	Friday

WEEK OF _____	Monday	Tuesday
SUBJECT:		

Wednesday	Thursday	Friday

WEEK OF _____	Monday	Tuesday
SUBJECT:		

Wednesday	Thursday	Friday

WEEK OF _____	Monday	Tuesday
SUBJECT:		

Wednesday	Thursday	Friday

May 2019

SUNDAY	MONDAY	TUESDAY	WEDNESDAY
			1
5 *Cinco de Mayo*	6	7	8
12 MOTHER'S DAY	13	14	15
19	20	21	22
26	27 MEMORIAL DAY	28	29

[Keep your eyes on the stars, and your feet on the ground. - Theodore Roosevelt]

THURSDAY	FRIDAY	SATURDAY	NOTES
2	3	4	
9	10	11	
16	17	18	
23	24	25	
30 *Water a flower Day*	31		

WEEK OF _____	Monday	Tuesday
SUBJECT:		

Wednesday	Thursday	Friday

WEEK OF _____	Monday	Tuesday
SUBJECT:		

Wednesday	Thursday	Friday

WEEK OF_____	Monday	Tuesday
SUBJECT:		

Wednesday	Thursday	Friday

WEEK OF _____	Monday	Tuesday
SUBJECT:		

Wednesday	Thursday	Friday

WEEK OF _____	Monday	Tuesday
SUBJECT:		

Wednesday	Thursday	Friday

june 2019

SUNDAY	MONDAY	TUESDAY	WEDNESDAY
2	3	4	5
9	10	11	12
16	17	18	19
FATHER'S DAY 23 / 30	24	25	26

[Adventure is worthwhile in itself.
- Amelia Earhart]

THURSDAY	FRIDAY	SATURDAY	NOTES
		1	
6	7 *National Donut Day*	8	
13	14 FLAG DAY	15	
20	21	22	
27	28	29	

WEEK OF _____	Monday	Tuesday
SUBJECT:		

Wednesday	Thursday	Friday

WEEK OF _____	Monday	Tuesday
SUBJECT:		

Wednesday	Thursday	Friday

WEEK OF _____	Monday	Tuesday
SUBJECT:		

Wednesday	Thursday	Friday

WEEK OF _____	Monday	Tuesday
SUBJECT:		

Wednesday	Thursday	Friday

STUDENT BIRTHDAYS

January	February	March

July	August	September

April	May	June

October	November	December

TEACHING IS A WORK OF

♡ *heart*

Made in the USA
Lexington, KY
05 August 2018